My Happy Black Teacher Journal

JOHNETTA MOORE

© Copyright 2021 by Johnetta Moore.

All rights reserved.

Printed in the United States of America on acid-free paper. All rights reserved. No part of this book may be reproduced or transmitted in any means or form by any electronic or mechanical including photocopying and recording, or by any information storage and retrieval system. Library of Congress Cataloging-in-Publication Data.

Johnetta Moore. My Happy Black Teacher Journal
Paperback ISBN 13: 978-0-578-87751-8
p.cm. (alk. paper)

Printed in the United States of America.

Cover Art by Shai Smith and Qhira Bonds
Book Typesetting by Nikiea

This journal is dedicated
to the people who continue to
make the biggest impact.

To my mom for your hard work, tough love, and perseverance.

To my sister and best friend for your unshakable guidance, and encouragement.

To my brother for your consistent communication and motivation.

To the black teachers of Macon, GA for your firmness, professionalism, and grace.

To my village of family, friends, and educators for your patience and advice.

To my three courageous, creative, and ambitious puzzle pieces for your existence that gives me purpose.

To my husband for your unwavering support, love, and devotion.

"If there is a book that you want to read,
but it hasn't been written yet,
you must be the one to write it."

- TONI MORRISON -

About this Journal

Your happy black teacher journal consists of reflection sections for 100 days. The next two pages will outline the sections in greater detail so you can get the most out of using your journal and daily practices of self-reflection.

Glows Section

Glows are the positive things: what you are proud of, the interactions that felt positive, or what you want to keep doing more of moving forward.

Examples of glows:
- a lesson that you perfectly
- a compliment from a colleague
- an accomplishment of a student

Grows Section

Grows are not quite opposite of glows: what do you want to improve, the moments that you felt unsure, or what you want to change or replace.

Examples of grows:
- a moment of anxiety
- a looming deadline
- an unannounced evaluation

The grows and glows sections of your journal is a place where you can reflect on your daily teacher practices. It is essential to have a positive mindset while you allow yourself to write freely. Practicing this daily activity will get you into the habit of focusing first on the positive things that make you a happy black teacher. Make sure you put the date!

I Matter Section

The I matter section features quotes to get your mind engaged on African Americans who made significant statements about education or positive mindset. In this section, you should write about your teacher philosophy, short term goals, long term goals, business ideas, dreams and much more. Use the I matter space to delve deeper into your legacy as a happy teacher.

Sample Page

Grows and Glows

Date: _____

Today, I am thankful for my Glows:

_____
_____

Today, I am reflecting on my Grows:

_____
_____

Quotes and I Matter

{ _____ }

Date: _____

I matter because…

_____
_____

Have fun journaling and outlining
your happiness as a black teacher.

Glows and Grows

Date: _____

Today, I am thankful for my Glows:

_____

_____

_____

_____

_____

_____

_____

Today, I am reflecting on my Grows:

_____

_____

_____

_____

_____

_____

_____

Date: _____

Today, I am thankful for my Glows:

_____

_____

_____

_____

_____

_____

_____

Today, I am reflecting on my Grows:

_____

_____

_____

_____

_____

_____

_____

Date: _____

Today, I am thankful for my Glows:

_____

_____

_____

_____

_____

_____

_____

Today, I am reflecting on my Grows:

_____

_____

_____

_____

_____

_____

_____

Date: _____

Today, I am thankful for my Glows:

_____
_____
_____
_____
_____
_____
_____
_____

Today, I am reflecting on my Grows:

_____
_____
_____
_____
_____
_____
_____
_____

Date:

Today, I am thankful for my Glows:

_____
_____
_____
_____
_____
_____
_____
_____

Today, I am reflecting on my Grows:

_____
_____
_____
_____
_____
_____
_____
_____

Date:

Today, I am thankful for my Glows:

_____

_____

_____

_____

_____

_____

_____

_____

Today, I am reflecting on my Grows:

_____

_____

_____

_____

_____

_____

_____

_____

Date:

Today, I am thankful for my Glows:

_____
_____
_____
_____
_____
_____
_____
_____

Today, I am reflecting on my Grows:

_____
_____
_____
_____
_____
_____
_____
_____

Date:

Today, I am thankful for my Glows:

_____

_____

_____

_____

_____

_____

_____

_____

Today, I am reflecting on my Grows:

_____

_____

_____

_____

_____

_____

_____

_____

Date:

Today, I am thankful for my Glows:

_____
_____
_____
_____
_____
_____
_____
_____

Today, I am reflecting on my Grows:

_____
_____
_____
_____
_____
_____
_____
_____

Date:

Today, I am thankful for my Glows:

_____
_____
_____
_____
_____
_____
_____
_____

Today, I am reflecting on my Grows:

_____
_____
_____
_____
_____
_____
_____
_____

Date:

Today, I am thankful for my Glows:

_____
_____
_____
_____
_____
_____
_____
_____

Today, I am reflecting on my Grows:

_____
_____
_____
_____
_____
_____
_____
_____

Date:

Today, I am thankful for my Glows:

_____

_____

_____

_____

_____

_____

_____

Today, I am reflecting on my Grows:

_____

_____

_____

_____

_____

_____

_____

Date: _____

Today, I am thankful for my Glows:

_____

_____

_____

_____

_____

_____

_____

_____

Today, I am reflecting on my Grows:

_____

_____

_____

_____

_____

_____

_____

_____

Date: _____

Today, I am thankful for my Glows:

_____
_____
_____
_____
_____
_____
_____
_____

Today, I am reflecting on my Grows:

_____
_____
_____
_____
_____
_____
_____
_____

Date: _____

Today, I am thankful for my Glows:

_____

_____

_____

_____

_____

_____

_____

_____

Today, I am reflecting on my Grows:

_____

_____

_____

_____

_____

_____

_____

_____

Date: _____

Today, I am thankful for my Glows:

_____

_____

_____

_____

_____

_____

_____

Today, I am reflecting on my Grows:

_____

_____

_____

_____

_____

_____

_____

Date: _____

Today, I am thankful for my Glows:

_____

_____

_____

_____

_____

_____

_____

_____

Today, I am reflecting on my Grows:

_____

_____

_____

_____

_____

_____

_____

_____

Date:

Today, I am thankful for my Glows:

_____

_____

_____

_____

_____

_____

_____

_____

Today, I am reflecting on my Grows:

_____

_____

_____

_____

_____

_____

_____

_____

Date:

Today, I am thankful for my Glows:

_____
_____
_____
_____
_____
_____
_____
_____

Today, I am reflecting on my Grows:

_____
_____
_____
_____
_____
_____
_____
_____

Date:

Today, I am thankful for my Glows:

_____

_____

_____

_____

_____

_____

_____

Today, I am reflecting on my Grows:

_____

_____

_____

_____

_____

_____

_____

Date:

Today, I am thankful for my Glows:

_____
_____
_____
_____
_____
_____
_____
_____

Today, I am reflecting on my Grows:

_____
_____
_____
_____
_____
_____
_____
_____

Date:

Today, I am thankful for my Glows:

_____

_____

_____

_____

_____

_____

_____

_____

Today, I am reflecting on my Grows:

_____

_____

_____

_____

_____

_____

_____

_____

Date:

Today, I am thankful for my Glows:

_____

_____

_____

_____

_____

_____

_____

Today, I am reflecting on my Grows:

_____

_____

_____

_____

_____

_____

_____

Date:

Today, I am thankful for my Glows:

_____

_____

_____

_____

_____

_____

_____

Today, I am reflecting on my Grows:

_____

_____

_____

_____

_____

_____

_____

Date:

Today, I am thankful for my Glows:

_____
_____
_____
_____
_____
_____
_____
_____

Today, I am reflecting on my Grows:

_____
_____
_____
_____
_____
_____
_____
_____

Date: _____

Today, I am thankful for my Glows:

_____

_____

_____

_____

_____

_____

_____

_____

Today, I am reflecting on my Grows:

_____

_____

_____

_____

_____

_____

_____

_____

Date: _____

Today, I am thankful for my Glows:

_____
_____
_____
_____
_____
_____
_____
_____
_____

Today, I am reflecting on my Grows:

_____
_____
_____
_____
_____
_____
_____
_____
_____

Date:

Today, I am thankful for my Glows:

_____

_____

_____

_____

_____

_____

_____

Today, I am reflecting on my Grows:

_____

_____

_____

_____

_____

_____

_____

Date:

Today, I am thankful for my Glows:

_____
_____
_____
_____
_____
_____
_____
_____
_____

Today, I am reflecting on my Grows:

_____
_____
_____
_____
_____
_____
_____
_____
_____

Date:

Today, I am thankful for my Glows:

_____

_____

_____

_____

_____

_____

_____

Today, I am reflecting on my Grows:

_____

_____

_____

_____

_____

_____

_____

Date:

Today, I am thankful for my Glows:

_____
_____
_____
_____
_____
_____
_____
_____

Today, I am reflecting on my Grows:

_____
_____
_____
_____
_____
_____
_____
_____

Date:

Today, I am thankful for my Glows:

_____

_____

_____

_____

_____

_____

_____

Today, I am reflecting on my Grows:

_____

_____

_____

_____

_____

_____

_____

Date:

Today, I am thankful for my Glows:

_____
_____
_____
_____
_____
_____
_____
_____

Today, I am reflecting on my Grows:

_____
_____
_____
_____
_____
_____
_____
_____

Date:

Today, I am thankful for my Glows:

_____

_____

_____

_____

_____

_____

_____

Today, I am reflecting on my Grows:

_____

_____

_____

_____

_____

_____

_____

Date:

Today, I am thankful for my Glows:

_____

_____

_____

_____

_____

_____

_____

_____

Today, I am reflecting on my Grows:

_____

_____

_____

_____

_____

_____

_____

_____

Date: _____

Today, I am thankful for my Glows:

_____
_____
_____
_____
_____
_____
_____

Today, I am reflecting on my Grows:

_____
_____
_____
_____
_____
_____
_____

Date: _____

Today, I am thankful for my Glows:

_____
_____
_____
_____
_____
_____
_____
_____
_____

Today, I am reflecting on my Grows:

_____
_____
_____
_____
_____
_____
_____
_____
_____

Date:

Today, I am thankful for my Glows:

_____
_____
_____
_____
_____
_____
_____
_____

Today, I am reflecting on my Grows:

_____
_____
_____
_____
_____
_____
_____
_____

Date:

Today, I am thankful for my Glows:

_____
_____
_____
_____
_____
_____
_____
_____

Today, I am reflecting on my Grows:

_____
_____
_____
_____
_____
_____
_____
_____

Date:

Today, I am thankful for my Glows:

_____
_____
_____
_____
_____
_____
_____
_____

Today, I am reflecting on my Grows:

_____
_____
_____
_____
_____
_____
_____
_____

Date:

Today, I am thankful for my Glows:

_____

_____

_____

_____

_____

_____

_____

Today, I am reflecting on my Grows:

_____

_____

_____

_____

_____

_____

_____

Date:

Today, I am thankful for my Glows:

_____
_____
_____
_____
_____
_____
_____
_____

Today, I am reflecting on my Grows:

_____
_____
_____
_____
_____
_____
_____
_____

Date:

Today, I am thankful for my Glows:

_____

_____

_____

_____

_____

_____

_____

_____

Today, I am reflecting on my Grows:

_____

_____

_____

_____

_____

_____

_____

_____

Date:

Today, I am thankful for my Glows:

_____

_____

_____

_____

_____

_____

_____

Today, I am reflecting on my Grows:

_____

_____

_____

_____

_____

_____

_____

Date:

Today, I am thankful for my Glows:

_____

_____

_____

_____

_____

_____

_____

_____

Today, I am reflecting on my Grows:

_____

_____

_____

_____

_____

_____

_____

_____

Date: _____

Today, I am thankful for my Glows:

_____

_____

_____

_____

_____

_____

_____

Today, I am reflecting on my Grows:

_____

_____

_____

_____

_____

_____

_____

Date: _____

Today, I am thankful for my Glows:

_____
_____
_____
_____
_____
_____
_____
_____

Today, I am reflecting on my Grows:

_____
_____
_____
_____
_____
_____
_____
_____

Date:

Today, I am thankful for my Glows:

_____

_____

_____

_____

_____

_____

_____

Today, I am reflecting on my Grows:

_____

_____

_____

_____

_____

_____

_____

Date:

Today, I am thankful for my Glows:

_____
_____
_____
_____
_____
_____
_____
_____

Today, I am reflecting on my Grows:

_____
_____
_____
_____
_____
_____
_____
_____

Date:

Today, I am thankful for my Glows:

_____

_____

_____

_____

_____

_____

_____

Today, I am reflecting on my Grows:

_____

_____

_____

_____

_____

_____

_____

Date:

Today, I am thankful for my Glows:

_____
_____
_____
_____
_____
_____
_____
_____

Today, I am reflecting on my Grows:

_____
_____
_____
_____
_____
_____
_____
_____

Date:

Today, I am thankful for my Glows:

_____
_____
_____
_____
_____
_____
_____
_____

Today, I am reflecting on my Grows:

_____
_____
_____
_____
_____
_____
_____
_____

Date:

Today, I am thankful for my Glows:

_____
_____
_____
_____
_____
_____
_____

Today, I am reflecting on my Grows:

_____
_____
_____
_____
_____
_____
_____

Date:

Today, I am thankful for my Glows:

_____
_____
_____
_____
_____
_____
_____
_____

Today, I am reflecting on my Grows:

_____
_____
_____
_____
_____
_____
_____
_____

Date:

Today, I am thankful for my Glows:

_____

_____

_____

_____

_____

_____

_____

Today, I am reflecting on my Grows:

_____

_____

_____

_____

_____

_____

_____

Date:

Today, I am thankful for my Glows:

_____
_____
_____
_____
_____
_____
_____

Today, I am reflecting on my Grows:

_____
_____
_____
_____
_____
_____
_____

Date: _____

Today, I am thankful for my Glows:

_____
_____
_____
_____
_____
_____
_____
_____

Today, I am reflecting on my Grows:

_____
_____
_____
_____
_____
_____
_____
_____

Date: _____

Today, I am thankful for my Glows:

_____
_____
_____
_____
_____
_____
_____
_____

Today, I am reflecting on my Grows:

_____
_____
_____
_____
_____
_____
_____
_____

Date:

Today, I am thankful for my Glows:

_____
_____
_____
_____
_____
_____
_____
_____

Today, I am reflecting on my Grows:

_____
_____
_____
_____
_____
_____
_____
_____

Date:

Today, I am thankful for my Glows:

_____
_____
_____
_____
_____
_____
_____
_____

Today, I am reflecting on my Grows:

_____
_____
_____
_____
_____
_____
_____
_____

Date:

Today, I am thankful for my Glows:

_____
_____
_____
_____
_____
_____
_____
_____

Today, I am reflecting on my Grows:

_____
_____
_____
_____
_____
_____
_____
_____

Date:

Today, I am thankful for my Glows:

_____

_____

_____

_____

_____

_____

_____

Today, I am reflecting on my Grows:

_____

_____

_____

_____

_____

_____

_____

Date:

Today, I am thankful for my Glows:

_____
_____
_____
_____
_____
_____
_____
_____

Today, I am reflecting on my Grows:

_____
_____
_____
_____
_____
_____
_____
_____

Date:

Today, I am thankful for my Glows:

_____
_____
_____
_____
_____
_____
_____
_____

Today, I am reflecting on my Grows:

_____
_____
_____
_____
_____
_____
_____
_____

Date:

Today, I am thankful for my Glows:

_____
_____
_____
_____
_____
_____
_____
_____

Today, I am reflecting on my Grows:

_____
_____
_____
_____
_____
_____
_____
_____

Date:

Today, I am thankful for my Glows:

_____

_____

_____

_____

_____

_____

_____

_____

Today, I am reflecting on my Grows:

_____

_____

_____

_____

_____

_____

_____

_____

Date: _____

Today, I am thankful for my Glows:

_____

_____

_____

_____

_____

_____

_____

_____

Today, I am reflecting on my Grows:

_____

_____

_____

_____

_____

_____

_____

_____

Date: _____

Today, I am thankful for my Glows:

_____

_____

_____

_____

_____

_____

_____

Today, I am reflecting on my Grows:

_____

_____

_____

_____

_____

_____

_____

Date:

Today, I am thankful for my Glows:

_____
_____
_____
_____
_____
_____
_____
_____

Today, I am reflecting on my Grows:

_____
_____
_____
_____
_____
_____
_____
_____

Date:

Today, I am thankful for my Glows:

_____

_____

_____

_____

_____

_____

_____

Today, I am reflecting on my Grows:

_____

_____

_____

_____

_____

_____

_____

Date:

Today, I am thankful for my Glows:

_____
_____
_____
_____
_____
_____
_____
_____

Today, I am reflecting on my Grows:

_____
_____
_____
_____
_____
_____
_____
_____

Date:

Today, I am thankful for my Glows:

_____

_____

_____

_____

_____

_____

_____

Today, I am reflecting on my Grows:

_____

_____

_____

_____

_____

_____

_____

Date:

Today, I am thankful for my Glows:

_____
_____
_____
_____
_____
_____
_____
_____

Today, I am reflecting on my Grows:

_____
_____
_____
_____
_____
_____
_____
_____

Date:

Today, I am thankful for my Glows:

_____

_____

_____

_____

_____

_____

_____

_____

Today, I am reflecting on my Grows:

_____

_____

_____

_____

_____

_____

_____

_____

Date:

Today, I am thankful for my Glows:

_____

_____

_____

_____

_____

_____

_____

_____

Today, I am reflecting on my Grows:

_____

_____

_____

_____

_____

_____

_____

_____

I Matter

I Matter Section
Famous Quotes that are near and dear to me. Enjoy!

"I am what time, circumstance, history, have made of me, certainly, but I am also, much more than that. So are we all."

- JAMES BALDWIN -

" Every great dream begins with a dreamer. Always remember, you have within you the strength, the patience, and the passion to reach for the stars to change the world."

- HARRIET TUBMAN -

"It is not light we need, but fire…not the gentle shower, but thunder. We need the storm, the whirlwind, and the earthquake."

- FREDERICK DOUGLASS -

"Life is only about the I-tried-to-do. I don't mind the failure but I can't imagine that I'd forgive myself if I didn't try."

- NIKKI GIOVANNI -

"I have learned over the years that when one's mind is made up, this diminishes fear. Knowing what must be done does away with fear."

- ROSA PARKS -

"One isn't necessarily born with courage; one is born with potential. Without courage, we cannot practice any virtue consistently."

- MAYA ANGELOU -

"Education and work are the levers to uplift a people."

— W. E. B. DU BOIS —

"Hold fast to dreams, for if dreams die,
life is a broken winged bird that cannot fly."

— LANGSTON HUGHES —

"We all have dreams. In order to make dreams come into reality, it takes an awful lot of determination, dedication, self-discipline and effort."

— JESSE OWENS —

"Just don't give up what you're trying to do. Where there is love and inspiration, I don't think you can go wrong."

— ELLA FITZGERALD —

"Change will not come if we wait for some other person or some other time. We are the ones we've been waiting for. We are the change that we seek."

— BARACK OBAMA —

"If you have no confidence in self, you are twice defeated in the race of life."

— MARCUS GARVEY —

"If they don't give you a seat at the table, bring a folding chair."

— SHIRLEY CHISHOLM —

INSERT QUOTE:

{ }

Date: _____

I matter because…

_____
_____
_____
_____
_____
_____
_____
_____
_____
_____
_____
_____

INSERT QUOTE:

{ }

Date: _____

I matter **because...**

_____
_____
_____
_____
_____
_____
_____
_____
_____
_____
_____
_____
_____
_____

INSERT QUOTE:

{ }

Date: _____

I matter **because...**

_____
_____
_____
_____
_____
_____
_____
_____
_____
_____
_____
_____
_____

INSERT QUOTE:

{   }

Date: _____

I matter **because...**

_____
_____
_____
_____
_____
_____
_____
_____
_____
_____
_____
_____
_____

INSERT QUOTE:

{ }

Date: _____

I matter because…

_____
_____
_____
_____
_____
_____
_____
_____
_____
_____
_____
_____
_____

INSERT QUOTE:

{ }

Date: _____

I matter because…

_____
_____
_____
_____
_____
_____
_____
_____
_____
_____
_____
_____
_____

INSERT QUOTE:

{ }

Date: _____

I matter **because...**

_____
_____
_____
_____
_____
_____
_____
_____
_____
_____
_____
_____
_____

INSERT QUOTE:

{ }

Date: _____

I matter because…

_____
_____
_____
_____
_____
_____
_____
_____
_____
_____
_____
_____
_____
_____

INSERT QUOTE:

{ }

Date: _____

I matter because…

_____
_____
_____
_____
_____
_____
_____
_____
_____
_____
_____
_____
_____
_____

INSERT QUOTE:

{ }

Date: _____

I matter because...

_____
_____
_____
_____
_____
_____
_____
_____
_____
_____
_____
_____
_____

INSERT QUOTE:

{ }

Date: _____

I matter because...

_____
_____
_____
_____
_____
_____
_____
_____
_____
_____
_____
_____
_____

INSERT QUOTE:

{   }

Date: _____

I matter **because...**

_____
_____
_____
_____
_____
_____
_____
_____
_____
_____
_____
_____
_____
_____
_____

INSERT QUOTE:

{ }

Date: _____

I matter because…

_____
_____
_____
_____
_____
_____
_____
_____
_____
_____
_____
_____
_____

INSERT QUOTE:

{ }

Date: _____

I matter because…

_____
_____
_____
_____
_____
_____
_____
_____
_____
_____
_____
_____
_____
_____
_____

INSERT QUOTE:

{ }

Date: _____

I matter because…

_____
_____
_____
_____
_____
_____
_____
_____
_____
_____
_____
_____
_____
_____

INSERT QUOTE:

{ }

Date: _____

I matter because…

_____
_____
_____
_____
_____
_____
_____
_____
_____
_____
_____
_____
_____
_____
_____

INSERT QUOTE:

{   }

Date: _____

I matter **because...**

_____
_____
_____
_____
_____
_____
_____
_____
_____
_____
_____
_____
_____

INSERT QUOTE:

{ }

Date: _____

I matter because…

_____
_____
_____
_____
_____
_____
_____
_____
_____
_____
_____
_____
_____

INSERT QUOTE:

{ }

Date: _____

I matter because…

_____

_____

_____

_____

_____

_____

_____

_____

_____

_____

_____

_____

INSERT QUOTE:

{   }

Date: _____

I matter because...

_____
_____
_____
_____
_____
_____
_____
_____
_____
_____
_____
_____

INSERT QUOTE:

{ }

Date: _____

I matter because...

_____
_____
_____
_____
_____
_____
_____
_____
_____
_____
_____
_____
_____

INSERT QUOTE:

{ }

Date: _____

I matter **because…**

_____
_____
_____
_____
_____
_____
_____
_____
_____
_____
_____
_____
_____

INSERT QUOTE:

{ }

Date: _____

I matter because...

_____
_____
_____
_____
_____
_____
_____
_____
_____
_____
_____
_____

INSERT QUOTE:

{ }

Date: _____

I matter **because…**

_____
_____
_____
_____
_____
_____
_____
_____
_____
_____
_____
_____
_____

INSERT QUOTE:

{ }

Date: _____

I matter because…

_____
_____
_____
_____
_____
_____
_____
_____
_____
_____
_____
_____
_____
_____

About the Author

Johnetta Moore is a veteran educator with over thirteen years of teaching experience in urban and diverse schools. She started her career as a special educator and later transitioned to an English Language Arts teacher. She has served in several roles over her tenure such as a Test Coordinator, Union Learning Representative, Mentor Teacher, Professional Development Course Facilitator, and Grade-Level Lead. Johnetta relocated to Baltimore in 2017 from Macon, GA. Since, she has launched Moore Learning Solutions, a tutoring company, and Freedom Dreamers Collaborative: a community based organization formed by four teachers to create spaces that see and value communities of color by providing tools and/or opportunities for students to thrive. She is currently working at a Baltimore City Public School.

Johnetta obtained her M.S. in Curriculum and Instruction from Georgia Southern University, a B.S in Business Management from Troy State University. Currently, Johnetta is pursuing an EdS at Liberty University. Johnetta is dual certified in English Language Arts and Special Education.

Johnetta's teaching philosophy is centered around a quote from Dalia Lama.
"Our prime purpose in this life is to help others. And if you can't help them, at least don't hurt them". Johnetta believes that education was her way out of poverty. She is deeply invested in helping students achieve regardless of ability levels, and she is most enthusiastic about making sure that all students are able to obtain a substantial literary education and feel like they matter in the classroom.

For booking and speaking engagements,
contact the author at **info@moorelearningllc.com**.

FOLLOW & STAY CONNECTED
www.moorelearningsolutions-llc.squarespace.com

www.ingramcontent.com/pod-product-compliance
Lightning Source LLC
Chambersburg PA
CBHW081940170426
43202CB00018B/2958